Other Books by James L. Adamczyk:

*A Eulogy For Man Anon*

*The Longing Road*

**James L. Adamczyk**

**Illustrations by S. J. Posselt**

**With an introduction by Phillip J. Adamczyk**

*First published 04/2018*

*ISBN-10: 1453717846*
*ISBN-13: 978-1453717844*

*Printed in the United States of America*

**Dedicated to**
**The successful establishment**
**of**
**Amoterra University**
**in Wisconsin.**

# *The Longing Road*

An Introduction

Few can claim to have seen it all; fewer still can claim to have lived it all. Within these pages rests a culmination and wealth of knowledge and emotion that reveals some of the greatest thoughts, struggles, joys, sorrows, and memories which define what it truly means to live the human experience. Our author brings to light not only his recollections, dreams, and imaginings, but also his unique perspective on the world.

I hope that you, the reader, may enjoy as much as I have unlocking and immersing yourself in the treasures etched down the *Longing Road.*

Each and every memory is a jewel of immeasurable wealth.

Spend them all wisely.

Cherish them forever.

-Phillip J. Adamczyk
Author, *The Chronicles of Terra* Series

# Part I. Organisms

(After Dr. William Harrold, UW -- Milwaukee)

## (The Only Poem I've Ever Titled) Untitled

When we cross
the highway bridge
over Butte des Morts
we will see
him casting from an old rowboat.

The sun may still be low in the east
but its reflected glare
hurrying across the water
will for a moment
swallow that lone fisherman
in brilliance.

He vanishes every trip
and we often wonder
if someone we'll never know
has caught any fish
since dawn.

S.J. Posselt

## The Race

Why are you running?
asked the little boy
in the alley
as I jogged past him
on mile number two.

A dragon is chasing me,
I replied, smiling,
at the corner
as I crossed the street
trying to catch my breath.

(He was still there when I came around again.)

I don't see a dragon,
he said, looking puzzled
on the sidewalk
as I slowed for his question
and a speeding car.

It's invisible, of course,
I told him, puffing,
by the mailbox
as I sprinted away
to the safety of the castle.

## Poetry

Poetry slowly deteriorates
nowadays
back into thought.

The Old rhyme and meter
long ago
rests on shelves.

Organic styles conquer
everywhere
the mind of modern man.

Sonnets' rhythms animate
nowhere
except in history.

Just the same, difference—
identity—
strangled by boundaries.

## Footnote On Life

This
is one of those Fort Devens days
almost,
cloudy in October;

it
reminds me of olive-drab places
past,
raining since midnight.

I
wonder about these gloomy moments
sometimes,
late Sunday afternoon;

why
should just a rainy day
suffer
for nothing it ever did?

## A Rainy Sunday Night

A beat cop walked past
in the rain
and I nodded to him
when he tipped his dripping hat.

The dog wanted to go out
in the dark
and I had to watch him
while he sniffed a hundred wet leaves.

Collage-colored trees shivered
in the wind
and like worn-out umbrellas
splashed me beneath them.

I returned home quietly
in the light
and poured a cup of coffee
about the middle of a good book.

I stared out the window
in the warm
and after the late news ended
dreamed close next to her.

## Night's Work

I fought magnificently
with my reptile brain
and Colt's machine rifle
in that dark jungle.

Twelve enemy caricatures
came across my sights
and are resting in pieces
because of our taxes.

Recoil—miss (again);
recoil—hit (down).
The ammo never runs out.
I was a good boy overseas.

## Observations On A Theme

I am
fresh paint for the fire escape,
watching some pretty girl
          walking past below

                    (Does the girl know?);

I am
steps and railings of old iron,
embracing a brick-red wall
          in case of fire

                    (Does the building mind?);

I am
high above the world, removed—
not even standing on the ground,
          but hanging

                    (Does the ground care?);

All that watch me back
are chilled drops of rain
          on the window sills.

## Second Encounter

In the beginning
there was dark.
And the dark was told,
"Let there be light."
And there was light.

And the dark saw that it was good.

Then along came man
one rainy day
and said to no one in particular,
"Oh, shit."

And the light flickered.

Man tried to extinguish the light
so that all might again be dark,
but the light slipped away
and returned to the stars.

It shines even now
and waits quietly
for man to look up and say,
"I understand."

## Picture Window in February

No sooner did I turn away
from some philosophy
and it was snowing,
prompted probably
by the west wind gone mad.

And then I turned back
and back again
and it had stopped
as though the sky were sorry
for what it had just done.

## First Snow, 1974

When the dog and I went out
I made her a snowball
and she ran with it
(as I chased)
so fast that she skidded
on the sidewalk
and shook and shivered
when I gave up.

I don't believe the grass
knew exactly what to think
of the two of us
as we dashed around
like kid and dog
who had never
never
seen snow before.

## Season's Greetings

Overseas near the end of a war
more than three ages ago,
we went out on guard duty
the coldest night of the year.

Tet's monsoon was our company
for thirteen hours straight,
and the wind wandered sullenly
across our muddy perimeter.

In the briefing they told us
to observe someone's cease-fire,
but the bunker was so flooded
we couldn't even sit down.

The truck with steaming coffee
found no willing driver,
and we had to wait for daylight
in miserable, dark vigilance.

When the morning came at last,
sleepy, cold, and silent,
we smiled and wished each other
a 'Merry Christmas' anyway.

## Down-Being

The loneliness of winter
becomes oppressive
a moment past the New Year.

Nights fill with nothing
but darkness
when the holidays are gone;

days are all afternoons
and usual
at least until March;

and people hurry away
in haste
to push and shove again.

If I were the Year’s end
I’d never
wait around to be martyred.

## Traveler and the Moon

### I

The moon and I talked
on the way home
late last night
early this morning.

We considered drinking
to ease the chill of winter;
studied sleepy dark houses,
debated the problem of routine.

All along the lake
we argued seriously
about icy intersections,
the government, and girls.

II

(I thought):
At least someone listens
with no unchanging notions
and seems to get along
even with countless stars.

(and)
A quiet, serious friend
is difficult to keep
when curling up is better
than sitting on the West.

(and):
Some prefer loneliness
at various odd moments
when there's no bother
to be anyone for sure.

III

The rusty old swing set,
missing a bar and chains—
but higher than the fence—
never said a word.

NEW
delicious
1001 uses
EXPAND YOUR MIND with
'BEARDED WALNUTS'
CRACK ONE OPEN TODAY
(YOU MAY BE SURPRISED!!)
a poetry anthology
UWM - fall '75

# Part II: Plastic And Performance

## (After Jim Hazard, UW -- Milwaukee)

## Night Wind

I listened to the wind
all night
last night,

shaking the awning
above twin windows
at the far end of my room.

It had pounded to get in,
like a vandal
testing the glass.

I turned over
in darkness
and listened quietly,

I'm safe, I thought,
smiling a little.
I said my prayers tonight.

## Who Said Patriotism Is Dead?

(After Vietnam, UW-Milwaukee, 1973)

I was walking
through the halls the other day
with my buddy Hate
looking for anti-war things
to rip down off bulletin boards.

Nothing.
Not a damn thing.
Thirty miles of corridors
and only
poetry
and a blood drive
and Veterans' dental benefits.

One might think
(I said to myself)
the war could get lost
before anyone gets a chance
to be all for it.

## Term Paper

When I went digging
for old poems
I found
I couldn't find any of them.

New old ones, I mean—
that might fill their space
in the latest retainer
(circular file?).

Would instructors understand
if I handed in
a collection of blank pages
of good poetry?

## Again

First snow this season that I have seen in Milwaukee: cold, dry. Very light. It doesn't stay. Never does.

In fact, as I look out it's still snowing. Windy. The grass in the neighborhood is all sparkly and white.

Odd. After a most unusual "Indian Summer," abrupt bitter cold. In 1940, there was a terrible blizzard in November.

Odd, too. The sun sparkles. I saw it over Butte des Morts. And the roofs, also, even in darkness. I see them now.

I wonder what becomes of the moon when nighttime prefers to happen beneath clouds. It's up there. Restless.

Good sleeping weather. Healthy. Keeps the covers on. The world out there: a big, frosty picture window. In here, quiet.

Well, time to read. Comfortable room, chair. Radio is quite clear because of the frozen air. Listen: Australia.

## First Snow, 1975

By late afternoon
to the west of the Lake:
flurries.

A good work-out.
I hurry from the gym
          to my car.

I remember
          yesterday's sunset.

By early evening
following autumn's retreat:
storm.

I study
          neighbors' yards.
White roofs, white grass.

I welcome
          warm, bitter tea.

The streetlight is lonely.

## October Night

Deep
the darkness
in the land
of the autumn moon,
where I
now standing
am eating
a last good tomato
from this year's garden.

Warm
the winds
in spite of October;
and I,
looking sideways
at clouds
that have gathered
since midnight,
am laughing.

Tired
the leaves
which interrupt
my thoughts:
I listen
But they are silent;
rusty curtains
scattering away
to earthy sleep.

THIS SHEET IS YOUR INVITATION TO:
!HALLOWEEN:
MADNESS: MADNESS*
YOU ARE INVITED TO THE CRAZIEST, MOST STUPENDOUS
COLLECTION OF IDIOTS THIS WORLD HAS EVER EXPERIENCED.
YOU WILL PARTICIPATE IN THE MOST GROSS, INGENIOUS, IDIOTIC
CRAZY, FILTHY, OBSCENE, BARE ASSED GAMES YOU EVER
SAW. BE FOREWARNED.
YOU MAY NOT LEAVE SANE OR EVEN ALIVE.
(BRING YOUR OWN BOOZE, FOOD AND ENTERTAINMENT PROVIDED)
WHERE: $1 PER PERSON PLEASE.
THE WIRTH'S
515 HAWTHORNE AVE.
S. MILWAUKEE, WIS
@ 8:00 PM SAT OCT 28.
515 HERE!
LOOK FOR MILLIONS OF JACK-O-LANTERNS
COLLEGE AVE
LAKE DRIVE
HAWTHORNE AVE
CREEK

# Winter Scenes

## I

I pulled the curtain away
to watch Tuesday's storm.

(to fall with the snow
through a dark morning
coming down
cold
very cold;

to lie a part of drifts
on some green-deep roof
sparkling
quiet
and white;

to wonder at the window
standing between scenes,
rigid
yet flowing
and clear).

I let the curtain drop
as an auto hurried past.

## II

Heavier now, falling fast.
And the wind!
Keep on.
Keep on.

Another eight hours
of soft violence
and surely
the city will have to stop.

See how careful it all is!
No need to justify
watching
just to watch.

## III

It is said
no two flakes of snow
will ever be the same.

I can hardly imagine that—
how many would there be?
More of them than people.

More than stars?

# Fire

Aw shit, said Mark.  It's raining.
I crawled out of the tent.
It sure is, I observed.
Our campfire was all but ashes
—hosed down nicely by the sky—
and the whole forest
faded away in every direction
into an early-morning mistiness.

What about breakfast? asked Jeff.
(A fire in the tent was out).
Eat it cold, I suggested.
Instead of a sunny, bright dawn
—given no choice in the matter—
the day arrived in clouds,
reminding all adventurers:
It's more challenging this way!

## (Some) Smoke

I slept
on the ground last night
out in the woods
—in a sleeping bag, of course—
next to a small campfire
and even closer to the stars.

I dreamed
a bear woke me up
to ask for some coffee
in an old tin cup
because he couldn't sleep
—I gave him some.

I woke
when the twilight of morning
shook me softly
—a reminder
that the glowing embers
needed fresh wood for breakfast.

## A First Impression

And you are going to be
a lawyer? –Hassan
You don't believe that? –me
smile
shake of head
i laugh
we both stand up
time for me to go
no parking-ticket worries
i act at ease
i cannot be touched
Thank you for your time –me
Oh –Hassan
walk, walk, walk (it's a long walk)
beautiful day, though
shit

## Summer Thunder

When I was a kid,
maybe twelve
            or thirteen
            in early August,
came that smell
            of summer-wet street
            during storm.

And I remember
crazy wind
            in the trees
against eerie flashes
            of night-bright sky,
like
someone taking pictures
only
with ten million flashbulbs
            all at once.

## Christmas!

If
you sit very quietly
    during snowflakes
on any night
    about Christmastime
you may suddenly feel it
—as a child might—
some
certain magic
which
can’t be quite found.

Don’t look for it.
The feeling
    is not to be held
but
simply to be enjoyed
    and wondered at.
It
is magic.

## New Job

Yellow lights (truck).

Guard duty all night
—security patrol, excuse me—
a long time.

Summer.
The freeway is never silent.

Blue dawn (morning).

## (Two Voices Tell Of) An Early Autumn

(With)
all that chilly rainfall
under
October's borrowed clouds,)

But
summer left us quickly
since
July had been too hot,

(Even
trees and birds and grass
puzzled
as seasons lost their way.)

And
by the dawn of autumn
we
expected jack-o'-lanterns.

## First Snow, 1977

Surprise!
Yelled Mother Nature
as she hurried off
into the north.

It stayed this time.

# The Fog

The fog
—delicate curtain
falling to whisper
that
summer's show
is ended—
came
for me alone.

# Part III: Times and Seasons (Life in the "Working World," After Both Vietnam and College)

## This Is Motor Truck Money*

It was a terrible feeling
back in those days,
and I remember it well:
not bad like someone just died
(because we had joked
that death would be a relief)
and not exactly permanent-seeming;
and I am not sure
if it was just the cold
or the bullshit we had to eat
along with our high wages,
or even if it was the effect
caused by living apart
and driving all those miles.

Anyway, it was to pay bills mostly
and enjoy life sometimes
while slowly and deliberately
becoming addicted to materialism
in a way that hurt only
when we had to think about it.

A waste, we said, of life—
of time, of smiles, of dreams;
but we all grew older faster
hoping simply for some out-of-sight day
when we, too, could retire
and trust Big Brother to provide:

despite our gray hair thinning,
legs walking with arthritis,
and bodies no longer well or capable.

That feeling that
we had to do what we did
because that's the way things are
and we have nothing to say about it
anyway or ever.
And we liked it,
I guess,
because we all stayed there
and did what we were told.

God bless America.

* A trademark of ADVANCE TRANSPORTATION COMPANY, 5005 South 6th Street, Milwaukee, Wisconsin 53215. The company went out of business in 1998.

## Season's Greetings, 1988

Again it is Christmas,
Still there is magic:
        light in darkness,
        warmth despite
                the north wind,
        and a comfortable quiet
                even amid winter's snow.
End-of-the-year holidays,
so special to children,
joyful but brief.
At such times,
we must all be children.
It is why we send, too,
our best wishes
        for the season.
They come with the magic.

## New Year: New Day

How shall I tell of such
simple things?
What would it take to make a Midwest poet
    of the upper Great Lakes region
    widely read and late-night enjoyed
    by those to whom poetry is
    just a bit mysterious?
Simple things!

Like this cold morning in early January:
brave brown birds at the cracked-corn feeders,
light snowflakes against high blue spruce,
a white-birch fire in the stove.
Simple things, yes.
A vacation existence in the deep woods
(perhaps as Frost must have imagined)
where technology is a new chain saw
and politics an overhead B-52
    just passing through
    on the way to Michigan.

And of religion?
That basilica sky atop stained-glass tree lines
with marbled floor of pine needles
    and forest litter
permits kneeling anywhere in the church,
no schedule of masses necessary.

## Today's Mail

It was an unexpected up
in a down-too-often world,
being able to say yes
to those people in California
who asked most politely
if they could publish
some of me.

Anyone might agree that
these patterns in the center of the paper
—we label them poems—
will forever be
as integral as my eyes or stomach
or some facet of my imagination.

Two thousand miles
is almost next door,
for my words were not spent
at the cost of time or distance
and never did I suppose
to consider them
in some perverse relationship to dollars.

What page do you suppose
they will put me on?

## They Must Have Thought (Vietnam, circa 1971)

Contrary figures
—are they not?—
these poets
who this moment
burst into tears suddenly
and then the next
as soldiers, too,
machine-gun one more enemy position
with mechanical precision;
who shudder
in almost-panic but then are calm
(worried
their comrades
might think them emotional)
as a dog runs the mine field
and disappears
in the sharp crack
of a dust-devil and spinning old tin cans;
who glimpse the fury
of a typhoon at evening
but then call it beautiful;
who run out with us
anyway,
bars of soap in hand,
partly beneath the roof's overhang
partly in the violent rain
to take a surely-needed shower
laughing
all the while.

AUG 71

## Ivory Towers

I did not mind writing poetry
while washing the dishes;
it was simply a confusion of hands
(and in the winter
mine used to crack and bleed).
One minute
stubborn food-bits beneath fingernails,
the following
a flurry of scribbles
for some profound assignment.
I would have done both
sans requests
and often did,
never wondering how much better
are soup bowls and baby spoons
than army pots and pans;
though I could have argued
(someday I may even
be really good at talking)
that inspiration
does not imply soap bubbles necessarily,
nor do State requirements
give us good teachers.
If it is not semantics,
then it must be some other rules:
nebulous
conversation
one-on-one
delivered

(I am not a betting man but)
I laugh to think
by some less-than-dynamic professor
on Sunday morning
while washing the dishes.

## Aryan Woman

(St. Cloud, Minnesota)

looking so hard
at a girl

so pretty
it almost hurts my eyes

and my face turns red
when suddenly

she looks up at me
and smiles

OCT • 72

## Field of Summer Sunshine

(For Phillip)

Little golden hair
and big dog

cutting through
the tall grasses

one stopping at odd moments
to collect red clover

the other
to snap at sand flies

like two different birds
eating side by side

each picking only
its favorite kind of seeds

## Many Miles Away

(For The Dragon)

Beneath that snow
(we cannot see them yet but)
there
are yellow flowers
rye grass and mosquitoes
a warm breeze
daylight-saving time
and even apples.

With a sudden heartbeat
dirty snow banks
along dangerous highways
must melt away
under the delicate kites
of April
until
(beyond dark days and cold nights)
summer assures us
it will be all right
to laugh again.

## Nothing Said

It was a silence
          born of silence,
of not knowing what to say:
child of discomfort,
lover of pride,
friend to no one.

Yet
as it rushed into our senses,
we all embraced
          that silence,
cheering it on
with the beating
          of our hearts.

Reflections

Watching her face
while in the mirror studying my own;
hurting, line by line—
she a child older
and I four years besides that.

We all travel this way,
I know;
not sadly,
but more properly
with indignation,
wanting to deny
having to become even one death wiser.

Might as well wish
it was always summer,
or Saturday afternoon,
or maybe Christmas.

# Part IV: Other Voices (Alverno College and Driving a Truck)

## In Re Oswald Spengler Et Al

I have wondered to conclude
there is a special affinity
between people and hills
—the cities are of little consequence—
in very early autumn
when most leaves are still just
thinking about a fatal posture.

It is an empathy
which becomes quietly apparent
in casual discussions
about apples and drought and red sand
and must here have something to do
with how big America really is
or used to be anyway.

Everyone gets a turn at greatness
—countries, I mean—
groups of people whose vitality
is entangled with pumpkin vines
and long strong rivers
and who stand tall momentarily
especially among the hills.

I have no choice, obviously
at being what I am but
from time to time wonder certainly
in a melancholy atmosphere if
—when my nation comes apart—

I also must feel embarrassed
and walk off bewildered, even bloody.

Yet there is an historical sense
of rejuvenation, of bright new worlds
which I often experience in almost-secret
—no doubt it is genetic—
when stormy winds like this build
and I look far beyond those hills
directly at the stars.

## Perspective

(On The Status Of The Late Federalist Government In America)

I watched them quietly:
those homeless people
who
with all their world
          packed into an old Chrysler
—three kids, four dogs—
(debt-ridden, I suppose;
without soap or water,
afraid of winter in Wisconsin)
were heading south
          on borrowed gasoline.

They wanted to know
if I would buy
          some of their belongings
because
they needed money for food and
—oh, yes—
asked also
if I might like
          one of the dogs
since
same were shelter-bound and starving,
not having eaten
in as many days
as had not the children.

## Christmas, 1989

Let us hope
—even in the darkest night
        of winter,
and no matter wind-driven snow
        at well below zero—
there will always be
that light
        in the eyes of the children
which tells
more about the magic
        of Christmas
than do all the stars
        in the sky.

Best wishes
for this holiday season!

S. Jo Posselt

## Slave Song

(To Be Sung While Working On The River)

There is a river in Hell, they say,
which all must cross on the outward way;
to taste its water makes one forget
and return to life with no regret.

I certainly made that journey once,
or more a thousand times, not once;
now here I am alive to think
but, wait—did I not stop to drink?

I still remember stories long past;
no mold was struck, no pattern cast:
trouble, sadness, terror, and pain;
the burning sun, cold autumn's rain.

One day King Cotton, I can see,
will sure have ginned even hope from me;
then he'll order my soul they deliver
to the shores of Styx, another river.

## Christmas, 1990

We can only imagine
    where the days have gone!
Delicate ornaments on old trees:
    glass becoming brittle,
    bright colors fading,
    snow sparkling in dark hair.
Winter is often now a sad time,
a place for secret memories.
Yet to watch the children
    lose themselves
    in holiday magic
is to remain assured
that life is far too short
for us not to live it
as though
    every day were Christmas.
Best wishes
for this Yuletide season!

## Nocturne of the Falling Leaves

It is you again, Autumn,
dancing darkly like some
peacock-colored windstorm
into the sadness of my heart.

Do not cover the world yet
with crying, dying leaves but let
me love your later flowers
for just a while longer.

Then dream carefully when you go,
for in quiet memory I know
there will ever ring the echoes of
sudden jack-o'-lantern laughter.

S.J. Posselt

## Thank You Note

### Which Might Have Been

### A Love Poem

It could have been infatuation
or perhaps just admiration:
watching this woman
with her unusual name
teaching them, teaching me—
inviting me to come closer.
We became to each other
microcosmic faces
in an ocean of expression.
If together we had been
in our own sixth grade
one semester would have lasted forever;
but now
the time is merely a foggy night
and we have become like
lighthouse and merchantman,
whose bright lights smile
at one another for an instant
and then are gone.

poems
Poems
Famous Poems
From Far and Near
Illustrated
By Michael

## Harbor Lament

Having heard them
from beneath my childhood bedcovers
they became part of
another memory:
foghorns in the harbor
on Lake Michigan.
I had to wonder
from where these ships
must darkly have come creeping,
(for never did I see them)
moaning in the distant mist
off Jones' Island.
It was there used to work
many poor Polish immigrants,
some of whom
must surely have known my grandfather—
though he worked in a steel foundry
with iron men during a happier time,
and whose own memories certainly included
those of polka-dancing
and drinking cold beer
on sunny summer afternoons
in a brand-new world.

## Out Back On The Hill

(In Memory of All Our Dogs)

What was left of all they were
went deep into the earth today;
down to ashes, to sand and clay
on a sullen Sunday afternoon.

They will be flowers in later spring,
away out back upon the hill;
almost sleeping and gently still,
not one shall mind the snow or thunder.

Our aspirations, too, must lie
beneath a troubled world, although
how high the near-by trees will grow,
embracing heaven with their open arms.

S.J. Posselt

## Epitaph For Grandfather Joe

It was to the graveyard that Thursday we came:
a collection of headstones, most quite the same;
a private retirement park of tombs—
but each with its section, flowers, and name.

I and my aunt had to visit him there
since this was, after all, the only place where
taxes and death could too soon be forgotten
(though my grandfather never really did care).

Many times then I would still have to wonder
what it was like to be sleeping down under
summer lavender and heaving, dark frost
with little concern for snowstorms or thunder.

While my aunt tore at weeds up near the tree
(she loved to manicure lawns, you see),
quite suddenly the morning began to rain
on the grass, the road, on my aunt, and on me.

Though my mind in poetic confusion was led
to verses concerning the life of the dead,
my aunt started running, shouting, "Let's hurry home!
I forgot to close the damn windows," she said.

## Lower Flat

You may at last move in some day
to be the girl up the stairs,
though
you might in fact be pretty
while
perceptive and mature—
perhaps
a student, or secretary.

And I of course will do my best
to watch you from the shadows,
since
you could at least be single
but
neither looking back nor free—
merely
a memory, or phantom lover.

…Still,
I would like to meet you.

## Minstrel Song

Ancient man looked up then dreamed
of stars; afraid, he was, of gods:
once upon a time now past
he climbed dark hills beneath a sky
filled with thunder, very high,
distrusting life (or so it seemed).

Modern man prefers to reach
for stars, in challenge, with ships of fire:
science and technology
define gods' lights as worlds and suns
too far to touch, too hot to hold
(catalogs list the name for each).

Future man will oft look back
and dream, though not of stars, but gods:
gone  away so long ago
of when (his laser disks will sing)
there were trees on gentle hills
and skies of minstrel blue, not black.

## New-Age Man

### (Mars: Landing Plus Three Days)

A desolation swept by sand,
a darkly crimson desert land;
a twilight nightmare, lit by fear,
asking us to ask, "Why here?"
Perhaps God's hand once filled her seas,
or held soft lilacs' scented breeze;
or fashioned mountains, strong and high,
toward blue-sky clouds just passing by.
But if that scene was manifest,
then long ago it ran to rest
on world whose look is lined and old
where water's far more rare than gold.
Though science and technology
were guides across infinity,
computers rule without a crown
should someone simply shut them down;
now outer space and fates we face
stand in perspective's proper place.
And when this expedition ends
(as even life its death attends)
—despite unpolished poetry
which none in fact may ever see—
I hope to travel home one day
so that at sunset I might say
my ashes, of whatever worth,
lie dreamless deep in Mother Earth.

## Dear John Letter

(Vietnam, circa 1970)

Just thought I'd write, my letter said,
to answer your last note;
and to mention (perhaps you've heard)
as of now…I'm dead.

I died around a week ago
while keeping guard all night;
I never had much choice or chance,
but when death stops—we go.

You said you found another guy
more perfect than the rest;
I was surprised about that news,
and sad enough to cry.

Well anyway, don't be concerned,
forget this foreign war;
I volunteered for Vietnam—
my medals all were earned.

Still, if one day I'm feeling better
(alive again, at least),
and have some time for nothing else,
oh, hell—I'll send a letter.

## For My Mother's Youngest Sister

Last sudden sunset startled me,
reaching out with mourning light;
it was another day gone dark—
thought death declined to hold me tight.

While all were there to wish good-bye,
instead my uncle caught the train:
that Outbound Special, Sixty-three—
without his raincoat, in quiet rain.

Now when I hear a distant whistle
sounded by some engineer,
oft and again I stop to listen
and feel, with sadness, a bit of fear.

I am turning old, I know,
carefully watching my children grow
in love with life as once I was
so many years, it seems, ago.

But after summer's sun is gone,
when ancient stars appear and shine,
the train departing will rush me up,
to keep those undone dreams of mine.

## Big-City Spring

Striving out of spring's sad earth
against a gray though thawing sky,
asking with innocence and quiet cry
for summer's promise of afternoon:
amazing flowers amid old brown
as rain starts fallin', fallin' down.

Just awake still looking back
at senseless dreams of drifted white,
memories now beneath the street
rush quite darkly to cold retreat:
endless journey in familiar town
while rain keeps fallin', fallin' down.

Silted gutters and salty rills
offset uncluttered silent trees;
at last that gaggle high but near
of geese whose daylight sense is clear
tears the winter's tattered gown
in rain that's fallin', fallin' down.

## The First Day Of Autumn

It happened with very early morning,
one while-you-slept affair,
like a pretty girl's
—in some sad love story—
        walking away.

Low-lying areas suffered most,
        as expected,
holding thirty-two degrees exactly;
surely the trees will now begin
        strutting,
September magic changing them
        to gust-torn rainbows.

This first afternoon should return
        brightly blue,
almost apologetic
for so many gentle green
        garden leaves frozen—
and a marshmallow campfire at dark
would not be
        out of the question.

## September Morning

Even this bright morning new
finds me dressed in old desire
as now are wearing for attire
my mind its memories, the east
its fire.

## Looking Back

(For A Lovely Lady Growing Old)

Affairs, like autumn's leaves, are brief:
our world gives nothing we may keep;
life is only a falling leaf—
day at sunset, the west in sleep.

## Across Late-Autumn Hills

(Wisconsin)

Memory alone holds ecstasy,
as footsteps vanish in fallen leaves;
October rain then washes free
that dust of summer along the lea.

Near-by farmers' sad-eyed cows
ignore this afternoon and browse
in broken fields of painful brown
once reserved for rusting plows.

Colors crumble to forest litter,
as eve's frost comes too soon;
and apples tell their harvest moon:
our wine is sweet, though season bitter.

## Ants...

Carpenter ants do not enhance
the worth or beauty of a home;
they chew good studs to honeycomb,
those dirty, rotten little ants.

Such dine on wood instead of plants,
eating holes in wall and floor;
leave it open-- they'll eat the door--
those dirty, rotten little ants.

I'd stomp them all had I my chance,
with boots or clouds of lethal smoke
to watch their numbers curl then choke--
those dirty, rotten little ants.

By the pyre's light they'd dance,
instead of waltzing in the grain;
I'd change their industry to pain,
those dirty, rotten little ants.

Some politician must advance
a law concerning bugs which eat
free lunch, but mostly-- I repeat--
those dirty, rotten little ants.

## Tradition!

(Christmas, 1991)

Darkness is deeper ever in the cold,
sadness always stronger sans the sun;
ancient Yuletide's here again although
Nature sleeps at senseless winter snow.

Shadows of some Celtic highland solstice
mellow aging moods, then memories;
magic warms the season's biting air;
children wonder, and scurry everywhere.

This—yes, this—is living's ecstasy,
faith that spring's tomorrow will be bright;
heaven's light, reflected in the stars:
given men, which now once more, is ours.

# Part V: Longing Roads (Three Worlds Together)

## Late Saturday Campus Afternoon

These falling leaves and growing old
suddenly tender pretty girls
who scold my senses with their bold
bright colors, blue-green eyes, and curls.
All are twenty, single, trim,
like one-time lovers in my life;
success to naught clear synonym
for stories I'd never tell my wife.
Such animated chivalry
would still resemble, I suppose,
some senior high school reverie
of chocolate syrup and pantyhose…
though hoping must amuse by that,
I quiet gray hair with my hat.

## A Family Affair

(For My Wife)

We've wound our arms about this world,
around these temporary selves;
our passion turned to blue-eyed sons
during summer's endless reverie;
but when have gone some hundred years,
what then is left of both of us
will grow together with the grass
which keeps a hillside quiet green;
for history's foundations lie
on famous deeds and opened graves,
while ordinary ecstasy
existence runs to bittersweet:
farmers in their fields of pain,
or heroes reading gilded books.

## Sunday Family Outing (1991)

Turning down that longing autumn road,
which seemed forever in its summer green,
I certainly gleaned attention for myself
by staring out: all so utterly yellow!
though I stayed most amazed, deliciously,
by such a perfect sun-filled afternoon
(surprised, like an archer finds surprise
at his arrow's sudden breakaway;
or like blue grouse startled by the hounds);
wondering as we stopped our car to look
if hurrying water below the bridge was cold;
for I stood lost then, pleasantly unbound
and until hopes or memories or both
were quenched by Phillip's ecstasy, who threw
a fist-sized stone into the silver river
—Christopher laughing one-year-old approval—
rushing with ripples away my secret dreams.

## Sea Fantasy

At how we met I hesitate:
these matters rather dress in chance,
and formal straits necessitate
a pseudo-distance with proper stance.
Still—our affairs I contemplate
in autumn daydreams about the sea:
my mind impassioned to create
lovers who revel breathlessly
on future sunset shores aglow
which, warm-wind soft, suggest our mood…
or have, perhaps, long years ago.
Yet what I feel in solitude
(your feelings quite unknown to me)
must not be hope—but memory.

## More Owed Than Earned

(After John Keats)

What little consolation, John,
at making meaning into rhyme
(assuming now you've wandered on
to more pastoral scenes in time);
for you might just as well agree—
with too-young final failing breath,
which awful message makes us see—
the consequence of life is death.

But that is all we need to know,
and that each work-long day brings rest;
love, perhaps, may last although
I feel we poets say it best:
this art, in truth, is agony—
lifeless immortality.

## Long Shot

Like the awful wrench of metal
torn beyond repair;
like some lover lost forever,
delicate and fair;

as lightning strikes a hapless hill
with dangerous disdain;
as winter rushes out in storm
to tender numbing pain:

my sniper rifle lies to tell
(it speaks for sadness well)
of better days ahead or past
(since wars but briefly last).

I hear while holding hot my breath
the sudden shout of sudden death.

## The Second Forty Years

How were we supposed to know
there someday would be others:
besides a sister or twin brothers,
children bright, and mothers?

No more (ever) me myself
or simply "two are one":
irresponsible's now done
while little's left to fun.

Older means "more easily"
is patently untrue:
skies of life oft fade from blue
for me, and you, and you…

## Mountain Epitaph

Now when what's final reaches close
to claim another—more than dear—
while we who live are left to mourn
a private winter drawing near;
then long-held tears dissolve anon
memories shared of many years,
since each needs ask if life is mere
such haunting pain, pervasive fears.

Still—there's a blue we've not yet seen,
for over sadness we will hear
that country quiet of vibrant spring
ignoring grief though offering
its crickets caressing their violins
and bullfrogs' music in the night.

S.J. Posselt

## The First Day Of School

Imagine! her crying
then hurrying on by
—a woman and mom I've never seen—
not wanting me to notice
such sentimental tears
at kindergarten's morning
(as if I
would never understand;
and me
just thinking poetry)
she besides not needing too
to be embarrassed
or considered ill-prepared
while certainly supposing
that men
don't worry, or cry.

## Veterans' Hospital

Its corridors twist a visitor
past barracks of quiet rooms
won by yesterday's soldiers—
heroes despite their bed-time uniforms.

Monitors could never indicate
tired hearts which still appreciate
medals once worn more proudly
than Medieval iron's heraldry.

Nor can nurses in pretty white,
though cheerful all the afternoon,
imagine some midnight enemy stalking
or battles now just foreign names.

Here veterans' combat options narrow—
for victory champagne long drawn
leaves empty glasses and faded thunder,
baffling daydreams and restless sleep.

## In Deference To Subjectivity

As once again I read their pages through
(this must be volume seven, number two),
I realize I'm scanning mostly space:
in poetry, white's never out of place.

Quite enigmatic scenes arrest my eyes
with language difficult to analyze,
and yet—how many pictures make one word?
Without being said a meaning's oft inferred.

The value of such art is not itself
(most books are sleeping on some dusty shelf)
but rather grows from art's creators—those
who write these special verses, I suppose.

When I was young and hardly knew the ropes,
I first put faith in skill, then lucky hopes;
for though I wrote profusely at that time,
I rarely thought to make things mean, or rhyme.

It really isn't what a person knows
(true—someone said a rose is still a rose);
it is instead who we might claim as friends:
they change our egocentric means to ends.

## Winter Afternoon

(Christopher and Sandy)

lounging about
lower flat of carpet

pseudo-cats:
new dog and second son

curled close together
all stiff and stretching legs

ignoring one the other:
each ever ready to run

## Summer Daydreams

Pigeons circled my old neighborhood
where as a stout grade-schooler I
played baseball in Pine Field
and rode my Schwinn through alleys
which outlined childhood's happier days.

At first there came those next-door friends
of every demeanor and size but,
later, some few favorite classmates
with whom questions about the world
got asked, discussed, and solved.

Seems now that years like pigeons rush
too fast away toward sunset,
and endless hot afternoons of summer
when I turn around surrender
to the snowy December winds.

## Autumn Garden

(You're Invited!)

Halloween is coming,
    its feeling's in the breeze;
the nights are lasting longer,
    Fall's painted all her trees.

The sun's gone on vacation,
    and clouds now congregate
to add their gloomy shadow
    in season growing late.

At last a sullen drizzle,
    chilly, gentle, cold,
varnishes the gardens:
    Nature turned to gold.

Come to THE

Halloween party

at Adamczyks'

Sat Oct 28 5 to 8 PM

bring your appetite

and wear A costume

Or e L s e

# Part VI. A Different World (Teacher, Custodian, Retiree)

## Human: Nature

The world waits.
Like a hungry big cat,
endlessly
the world waits.
With sleepy eyes,
during doldrums and drought,
the world watches;
despite crickets and April rain,
it listens.
And man (of all people!)
hardly appreciates
his tertiary attire:
the possibility
he might just be
some toy kept near
for the amusement
of a world which waits.
A hungry world,
a big-cat world,
always watching,
ready to play.

## Resume

Tires, trucks, and snow all night,
my life was longing roads:
a million miles of yellow lines
out, about, then back;
with kinesthetic highway signs
forever rushing by.

I kept no trees or summer clouds,
just crowds of noisy cars;
dirty waysides, no left turns,
police with quota sheets;
impressive paychecks every week,
and home on Saturday.

When tabs are taken after hours,
reflection well may tell—
in spite of job security
or pension benefits—
that all roads run o'er distant hills
to vanish in the sea.

S.J. Posselt

Yule 2004

In this tragic rush of days,
life's lessons rest unmet;
crumbling browns and gold turned grays:
the ages pirouette.

Once upon a Keltic time,
writ in summer's light,
runes which told of Nature's rhyme
lie lost in winter white.

Given charge to keep that light,
we send out greetings, too;
as Yuletide fires warm the night:
our best to yours, and you.

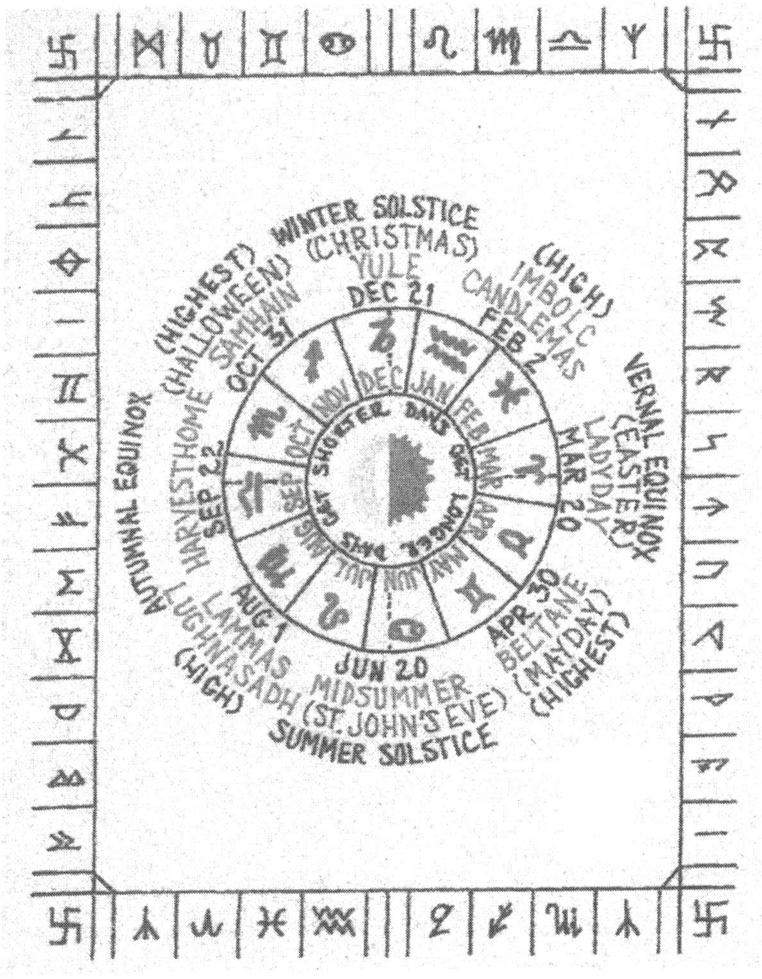
WINTER SOLSTICE
(CHRISTMAS)
YULE
DEC 21
(HIGH)
IMBOLC
CANDLEMAS
FEB 2
VERNAL EQUINOX
(EASTER)
LADYDAY
MAR 20
APR 30
BELTANE
(MAYDAY)
(HIGHEST)
JUN 20
MIDSUMMER
(ST. JOHN'S EVE)
SUMMER SOLSTICE
AUG 1
LAMMAS
LUGHNASADH
(HIGH)
AUTUMNAL EQUINOX
SEP 22
HARVESTHOME
OCT 31
SAMHAIN
(HALLOWEEN)
(HIGHEST)
SHORTER DAYS
LONGER DAYS

## Fire Poem

Writing poetry, you say?
Rhyming rhythm style?
Once upon a time I did,
without a smile, try.

Still I may someday again
set my mind to verse;
consider life and death, or love;
define our Universe.

For this moment now, and here,
imagination's spent;
Chaos came to reap, and so:
ashes in the snow.

## Yuletide 2006

An animated orrery
of apathetic leaves;
a hurdy-gurdy melody
of bitter, icy breeze;
the panoramic pirouette
of sudden velvet snow:
winter's silent solstice wears
its somber, sullen pall.

Still, Christmas is our antidote
for seeming entropy;
and ever better, always up –
never mind the years;
night's in dreams as day is born:
New Year here again!

## Elegy Written in a Nuclear Aftermath

The gravest show on Earth!
The end of the world
(well—not the *whole* world);
plus a scaling-back of taxes
            and welfare
            and Monday night football.
Biblical proportions, certainly,
with plutonium and fallout:
everyone versus everyone
in helter-skelter mode
absent any future hope;
one for all
            and all for no one.

This is, of course,
what governments do
            and have always done
for at least three thousand years
            or so, and so it goes
about nothing being new
beneath our restive sun:
which saw Egypt rise and fall,
the Church make warfare holy,
Kepler clarify the cosmic order,
Oppenheimer break apart an atom,
and Bush destroy the world
(well—not the *whole* world).
But close enough.

## Call of the Cowboy

Perhaps upon some long ago,
I should have been a cowboy;
strong and tall but dark and deep,
like John Wayne in those movies.

Now *here* was a real American,
advertised life-sized;
up-front Nature, close and dusty,
hard as Dakota dirt.

No fences or good neighbors near,
just range and endless sky;
one colorful moment in history,
a West which never was.

Then there's that famous final scene:
the good guy gets his girl;
the rosy sun goes down all red,
and happy ends their day.

Oh, I could have been a cowboy, too
(I can even shoot a gun);
strong and tall but dark and deep,
riding down the trail.

S.J. Passelt

## Christmas 2013

The icy arms of winter find
us missing summer's daze;
or walks through tumbling colored leaves,
or even pumpkin pie.

This world has taken many turns
in twenty-one hundred years;
still, Christmas offers fire and light
during Nature's darkest night.

**And our best wishes hope to see**
your season bright with cheer;
for sleeping spring must wake again
in the soon-to-be New Year.

## All Hallows' Eve, 2014

West wind is singing
its icy refrain,
as falling leaves swirl
and dance down the lane.

Forests in darkness,
moonlight in mist;
pies baked with apples,
a card game of whist.

Fields plowed and frosty,
wood cut and split;
that sharp  spicy cider
'neath cold starry sky.

Pumpkins and cornstalks,
the sweet smoke of birch;
whispers of autumn:
winter's anon.

S.J. Posselt

## Love Poem?

playing so hard
with a girl

so pretty
it almost burns my hands

and my face turns red
when suddenly

she looks up at me
and says "that tickles"

## Scandal

Rod hit that ball so hard
it landed on the Moon
bounced thirty times
(due to Luna's lesser pull)
and came to rest
in a cloud of crater dust.

The Cosmonaut who found it
shook his helmet and snorted
(thinking they can hit a ball
*this far*
-- damned Americans--
but still it goes afoul).

Nearby Grays could not appreciate
same situation
(never having played the game)
and so went about mining gold
hoping later to have more vodka
with their awesome Russian friends

## Christmas 2015

When summer too suddenly slips away,
and autumn's rainbow leaves have gone;

while north winds hurry across the sky,
with icicle-sparkling, pointed teeth;

as storm fronts rattle shutters out back,
and Yuletide fires crackle to life;

our world lies sleeping 'neath covers of white,
in regular rest from the rush of time.

Then cognac and cookies, the smoke of birch;
evenings come early, with spirited nog;

fir trees in baubles, candles alight,
and children off singing old holiday songs.

For best friends and strangers wishes we send,
hopes as high as stars in the night.

## Drivers' Education

A late October fog deceives:
as sleepy innocent rural roads
collect their silent phantom hoar
and then invite indifference.

Why, yes-- it was excessive speed,
while texting proceeded matter-of-course;
but now the high school three attended
will only just remember them.

A shame-- they were so young, they'll say:
forever fourteen, sixteen; so
we'll need to be more vigilant
when placing flowers along that stretch.

Well, what have we learned in class today
about life? Oh, nothing much at all:
a smart phone's faster than reading old books,
and writing comes *after* the football game.

## Stone Cutter's Lament

Who would chance to trust this world:
hearts are broken, milk is spilled;
things fall down and we grow old;
when even children move away?

Life's at best a wistful wishing
despite the contretemps of time:
disabled, homeless, rich, with fame...
in the end the end's the same.

It's there our aspirations lie,
it's where we all one day must lie:
tasting ashes, smelling earth,
resting forever below the snow.

Oh, no-- I shall not gently go
into that quiet awful night;
for I am wont to cross those fields
with fists held tightly-- left and right.

## A Brady Banana Bunch

Baseball, football, tennis, golf;
who *cares* if they can't read?
No lies, no cheating, move along--
we *know* it's just a *game.*

Religion on a grid of iron,
saints and angels, too;
one hundred *heroes* every week,
photogenic and true blue.

There is an elephant in here,
standing on my foot;
but then's the *game* at three o'clock--
with kegs of ice-cold beer.

America! America!
God turns His back on you.
Non-stop play with *lots* of balls,
and billions of bananas.

## Synthetic

She was a phantom of terabytes,
a silver lattice of sheer delights;
"ons" and "offs" of elegant affair,
sophisticated enough to dim the lights.

Why I needed her I cannot say,
as uniquely different were we two;
one silicon matrix, one carbon design:
honey and lemon, water in wine.

We could never have lasted, not at all,
random and separate as night and day;
for when that storm shut the power
down:
I ran, humbled-- she melted away.

About the Author

Jim Adamczyk was born in Milwaukee, Wisconsin, a long time ago. Home was the south side neighborhood of Bay View, where Jim attended and graduated (valedictorian) from Bay View High School in January of 1969.

Jim's subsequent endeavor found him a member of the United States Army Security Agency; his service time included one and one-half tours in the late Republic of South Vietnam.

Post service was spent taking advantage of the "GI Bill" to earn a Bachelor of Arts degree from the University of Wisconsin in Milwaukee, with the intention to pursue a career in Law or law enforcement.

Employment, however, included that as a private security police officer, dock man, and truck driver. While working for a trucking company in Milwaukee, Jim later returned to school as a non-degree student at Alverno College to earn a teaching certification in English at both junior and senior high school levels.

All of the poems included herein were written during the above adventures and represent many years of Jim's life's experiences.

93678451R00090

Made in the USA
Columbia, SC
17 April 2018